Durrell McKenna, Nancy
Kwazulu, South Africa.—(Beans)
1. Kwazulu (Natal)—Social life and customs
—Pictorial works—Juvenile literature
I. Title
968'.4'004963 DT879.Z9
ISBN 0-7136-2423-X

Published by A&C Black (Publishers) Limited
35 Bedford Row, London WC1R 4JH

Acknowledgments
The maps are by Tony Garrett

ISBN 0-7136-2423-X

Filmset by August Filmsetting, Haydock, St Helens.
Colour reproduction by Hongkong Graphic Arts Service Centre
Printed in Hong Kong by Dai Nippon Printing Co. Limited

KwaZulu South Africa

Nancy Durrell McKenna

Adam and Charles Black · London

My name is Busisiwe. I'm ten years old and I have three brothers and two sisters. We live with Granny because Mum died when I was very young. The place where we live is called Ekuvukeni. It's in the eastern part of South Africa.

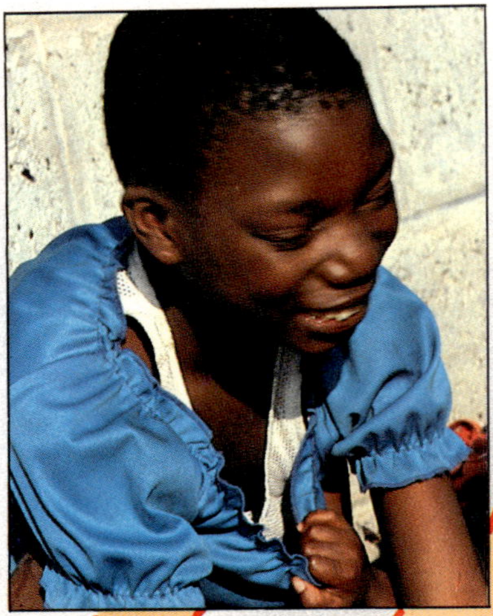

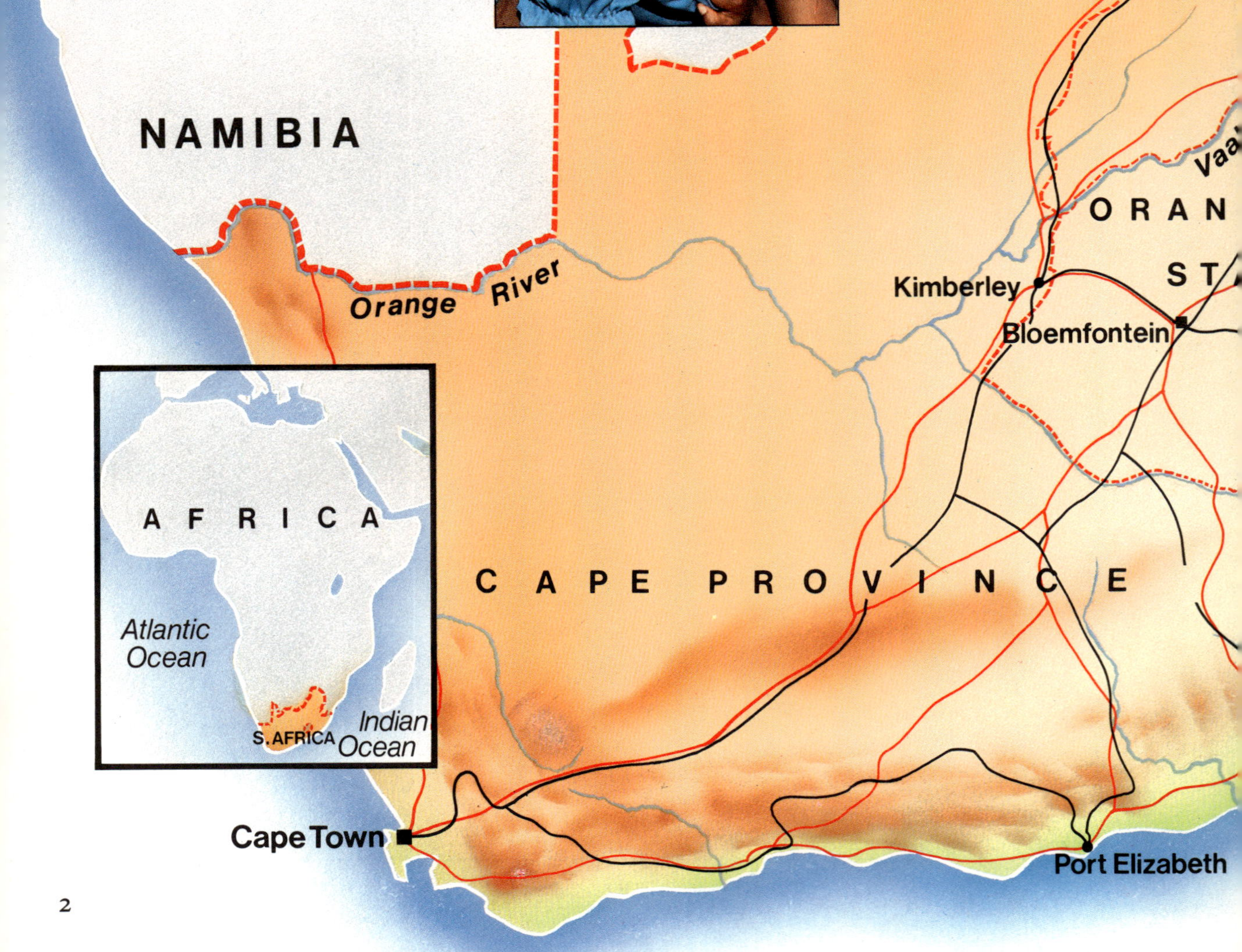

South Africa is divided into four provinces, Cape Province, Transvaal, Orange Free State and Natal. Ekuvukeni is in the province of Natal.

No white, coloured or Asian people live in Ekuvukeni. The government of our country has made laws which say that white, coloured, Asian and African people must live in different areas. We have to go to different schools and clinics and ride in separate trains. This system of keeping people apart is called apartheid.

My Granny's name is Thandiwe, which means 'The loved one'. It's a Zulu name. We are Zulu people and I speak Zulu as well as English. Granny is dressed in black because she is in mourning for her husband, Alfred. He died last year. Grandfather was an Anglican minister. He preached to us on Sundays and, during the week, he visited people who were sick or needed help.

Granny hasn't always lived in Ekuvukeni. She was born in a little village a few hours drive from here, near the big town of Ladysmith. Her parents were farmers.

Soon after Granny married Grandfather, the government passed a new law of resettlement. This law meant that my grandparents and many of their friends were made to leave their homes and move to Ekuvukeni.

Granny often tells me about the day they had to move. A government truck came to take them away from their home. It was very early in the morning and they had no time to pack. Granny and Grandfather had to leave almost all their things behind. They were only allowed to take what they could load on to the truck. Then they were driven out to Ekuvukeni. Granny says it was very dry and bare compared to her old village.

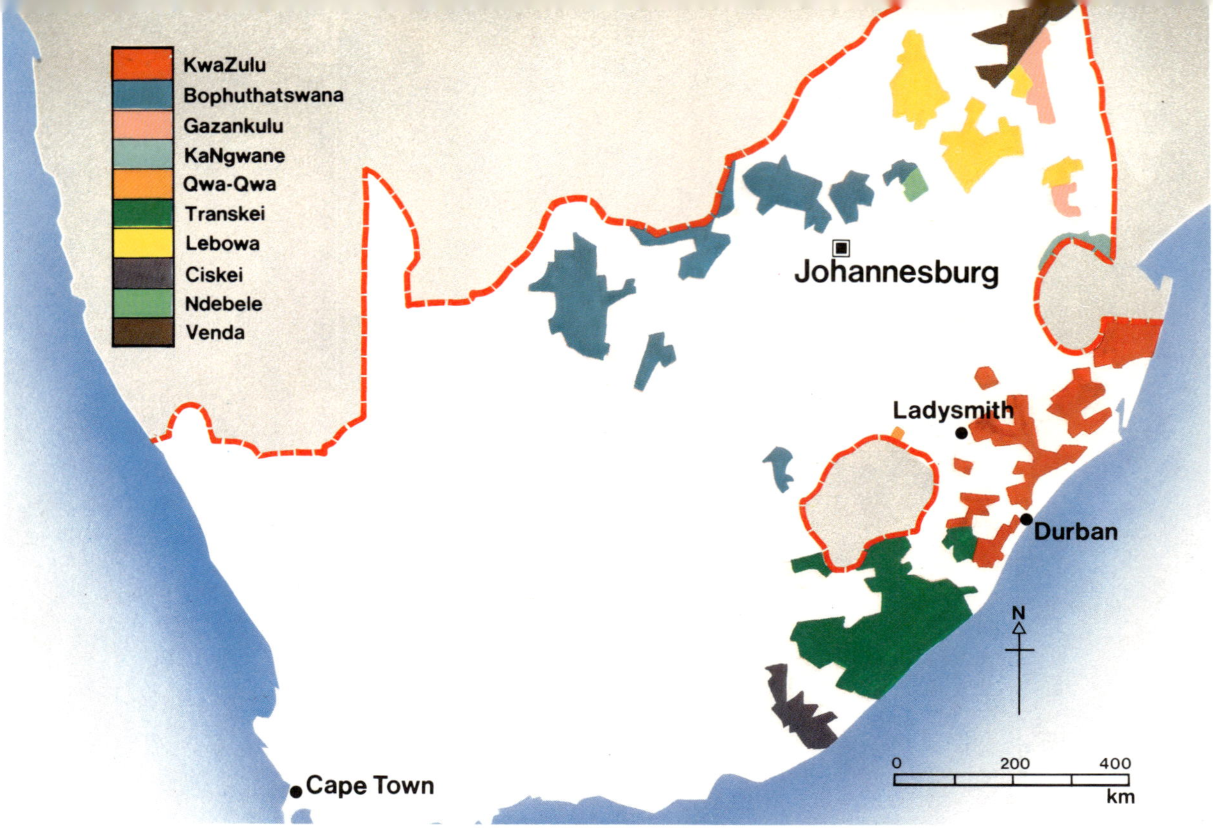

Ekuvukeni is in an area which the government calls KwaZulu. They say that KwaZulu is a 'homeland' where all Zulu people should belong. But Granny says it isn't home for her. There are ten different 'homelands' in South Africa. Each one is supposed to be for a different group of African people.

When Granny and Grandfather first moved to Ekuvukeni, they lived in a house like this one. It's made of corrugated iron and gets very hot in summer and cold in winter.

After a few months, Granny and Grandfather built a mud house. Mud houses are much cooler in summer and warmer in winter. But when it rains, the mud begins to crumble and it's hard to keep repairing the walls.

There are different ways of building a mud house. One way is to dig mud from the ground and cut it into bricks. Another way is to make two wooden frames about the width of a fist apart. Then you pack the gap with mud and straw. Our neighbour's house is being built like this.

This is the house we live in now. Granny is very proud of it and so am I. Granny and Grandfather built it with some help from a neighbour. The house is made of cement blocks which cost a lot of money. My grandparents bought the cement with money they had saved before they came to Ekuvukeni.

Our house has a living room, dining room, two bedrooms and a kitchen, but the kitchen isn't finished yet. I share a bedroom with my sisters and my Aunt Florence. Granny has a room all to herself. We don't have electricity in our house, so at night we use candles or oil-burning lamps.

Granny's old mud house is just next door. It has two rooms. Granny uses one room as a kitchen and the other room is where my brothers sleep.

We have one of the best houses in Ekuvukeni. Lots of our neighbours still live in houses made of mud or corrugated iron. Many of the men here must live away from home to find work, so the women have to manage on their own. They are much too busy to build new houses by themselves and they can't afford to pay for builders or cement.

It's hard to get a job in Ekuvukeni. There are no factories here and the land is too dry and sandy for farming.

Some people manage to get jobs in Ladysmith. Our neighbour, Mr Zondi, works in a garage there. It takes about an hour and a half to get to Ladysmith by bus, so he has to get up at four o'clock in the morning. But it means that he can live with his family.

Most of the men work much further away from home. My Uncle Sipho works on a sugar plantation near Tongaat. It is too far to travel every day, so he lives there for most of the year.

Uncle Sipho carries a pass book which says that he lives in Ekuvukeni and is a farmworker in Natal. In South Africa, all Africans must have a pass book which says where they live and work.

Granny has a pass book which says that she lives in Ekuvukeni. She has to take it with her everywhere, even if she's only going to the shops.

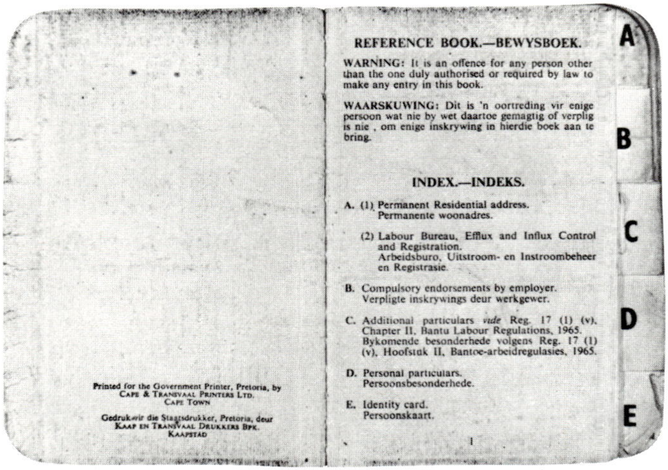

Printed for the Government Printer, Pretoria, by
CAPE & TRANSVAAL PRINTERS LTD.
CAPE TOWN

Gedruk vir die Staatsdrukker, Pretoria, deur
KAAP EN TRANSVAAL DRUKKERS BPK.
KAAPSTAD

REFERENCE BOOK.—BEWYSBOEK.

WARNING: It is an offence for any person other than the one duly authorised or required by law to make any entry in this book.

WAARSKUWING: Dit is 'n oortreding vir enige persoon wat nie by wet daartoe gemagtig of verplig is nie, om enige inskrywing in hierdie boek aan te bring.

INDEX.—INDEKS.

A. (1) Permanent Residential address.
Permanente woonadres.

(2) Labour Bureau, Efflux and Influx Control and Registration.
Arbeidsburo, Uitstroom- en Instroombeheer en Registrasie.

B. Compulsory endorsements by employer.
Verpligte inskrywings deur werkgewer.

C. Additional particulars *vide* Reg. 17 (1) (v), Chapter II, Bantu Labour Regulations, 1965.
Bykomende besonderhede volgens Reg. 17 (1) (v), Hoofstuk II, Bantoe-arbeidregulasies, 1965.

D. Personal particulars.
Persoonsbesonderhede.

E. Identity card.
Persoonskaart.

1

A B C D E

My dad works on a building site in Johannesburg, a big modern city in the province of Transvaal. It's a whole day's drive from Ekuvukeni, so my dad can't live with us while he's working. He lives in Soweto, a township just outside Johannesburg. Most of the Africans who work in Johannesburg have to stay in townships like Soweto.

Dad lives in a men's work hostel like this one. He comes home once a year at Christmas. We miss him very much, but Granny needs the money which he sends us.

Every day, Dad travels into the city by train. There are separate train stations for black people and white people, and different trains. Dad's station is always very crowded and lots of people set up stalls there to try and make a bit of extra money.
Dad says that you can buy almost anything at the station, from vegetables or live chickens to pots and pans. He often buys some food at the station on his way back from work.

Granny says it's hard to look after us without Dad or Grandfather to help at home. Some of her friends go into Ladysmith and look for work in factories, although not many of them manage to find jobs. Other women set up stalls on the street to try and earn money. But many of the women have too much to do at home, especially when the men have to be away for most of the year.

On weekdays, Granny gets up at six o'clock so that she can cook our breakfast before we go to school. We usually have mealie-meal, which is a kind of porridge made from maize-meal and water. In Zulu, it's called Iphalishi.

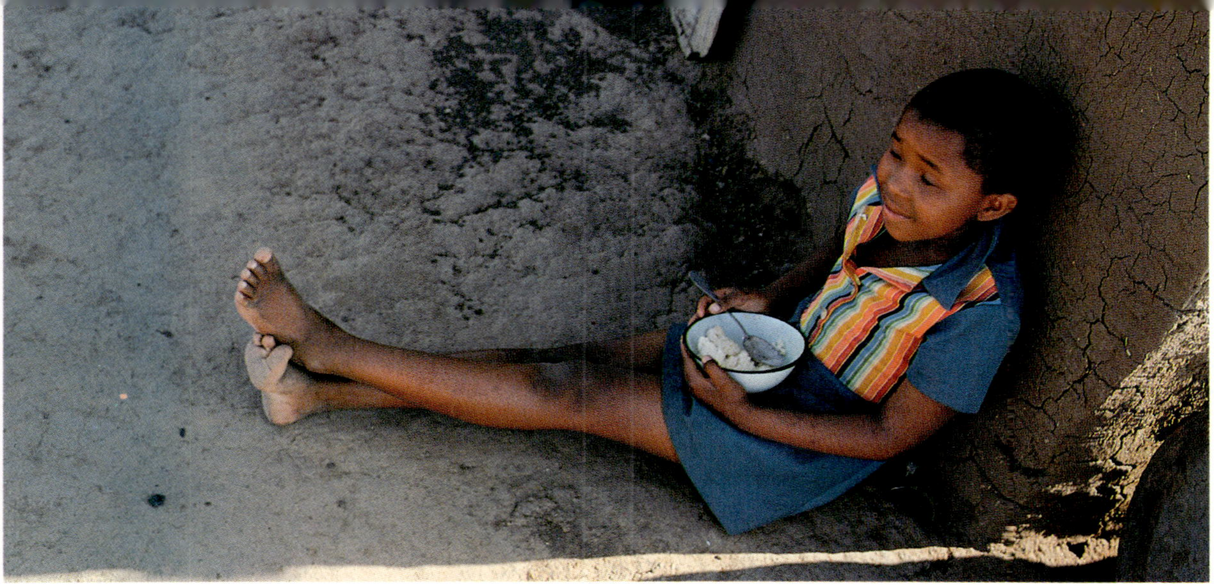

We often have Iphalishi for dinner, too. Sometimes we have pumpkin pudding, and on extra-special occasions we have a chicken. Meat is expensive, so we hardly ever eat it.

Granny does all the shopping. She buys most of the things we need from the local shop in Ekuvukeni. But if she wants to buy something special, like my clothes, she takes the bus to Ladysmith.

When I'm not at school, I try to help Granny with the chores. Fetching water is my most important job. In good times, we get water for cooking, washing and drinking from a tap outside the house. About four families share the tap. Here's my sister carrying some water back to the house.

There never seems to be enough water. Our summer lasts from November until February. It's usually baking-hot and very dry. When there is no rain, we have droughts. Then the taps dry up and we have to get our water from the government water trucks. The trucks can come at any time of day or night, so we must always have our containers ready.

Last year there was a drought further east, where some of Granny's friends live. Their taps were cut off for three weeks and they had to queue for water at a big reservoir. It took a very long time, because there were about five hundred people waiting.

There are lots of other chores to do. In the morning, the women do their washing and housework. Then they collect wood for fires and light the braziers for cooking. In winter, we also use the braziers to keep us warm.

Some of the women plant vegetables on their plots of land. Where they used to live, there was enough land to plant mealies and sweet potatoes, as well as to keep animals.

A few of our neighbours planned to start new farms in Ekuvukeni, so they brought their farm tools and machines. But there isn't enough land here for farming and the soil is so dry and sandy that only a few vegetables will grow.

Granny has organised a group with ten other women. They meet at our house once a week and teach each other new skills, like crocheting and making school uniforms for the girls. Last year they set up a workshop to repair bicycles and primus stoves.

I go to school in Ekuvukeni. It takes me about fifteen minutes to walk there and lessons start at eight o'clock in the morning. I finish school at one o'clock and another class has lessons in the afternoon. There isn't enough room in the school for everyone to have their lessons at the same time.

I'm in my third year at school. My teacher's name is Miss Lungili, which means 'a kind one' in Zulu. She writes our lessons on the board and we repeat them out loud.

My favourite subject is nature study, but we also learn Zulu, English, arithmetic and health and hygiene.

It costs Granny 15 rand a year to send me to school. This pays for a school meal for me and any repairs which are needed on the school building. My school uniform is expensive, too. It costs about 30 rand. I'm very glad that the women in Granny's group will be able to make my next uniform.

My brothers and sisters all go to school, too, and I'm hoping to go to secondary school when I'm older. But many families in Ekuvukeni can't afford to send their children to school.

Sunday is a special day for us. Granny gets up very early and boils some water for us to wash in. It's always my job to wash my little sister's hair. Then we all put on our smartest clothes for church.

When Grandfather was alive, he gave the service every Sunday. Since he died, we haven't had our own minister. Today, a visiting minister is coming to give us a sermon and Granny's ironing a fresh gown for him. She heats the iron on the stove and then cleans the bottom of the iron by rubbing it on the ground. It takes a long time to make the gown look just right.

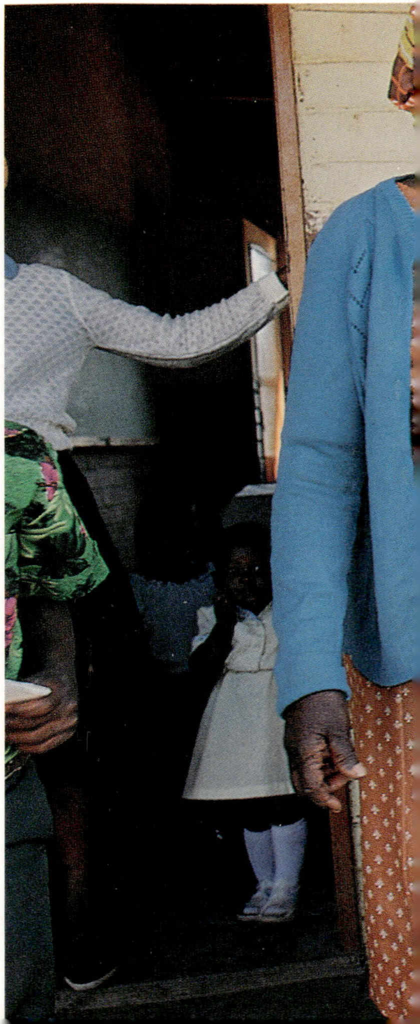

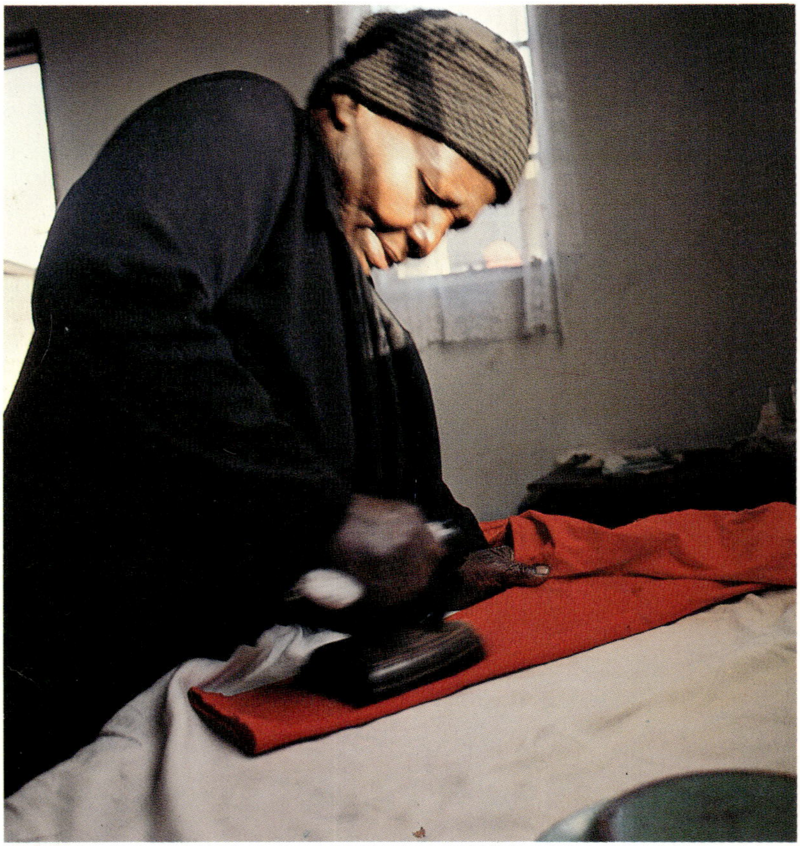

We don't have our own church yet, so we use the secondary school. When there is no visiting minister, the men and women in our congregation take it in turns to lead the service. I love singing hymns and Granny knows all the words. But sometimes now, she just listens. Perhaps she's thinking about Grandfather.

After church, Granny always stays to chat to her friends and find out everybody's news. Her friends are always pleased to see her and it makes me happy to see Granny laughing and joking.

In the evening when it's dark and only the candles are lit, I like to hear Granny tell stories about her childhood. Sometimes she tells us about the history of the Zulu people and the great Zulu leaders, like King Shaka.

We are learning the cheers of the Zulu people. My brothers and sisters and I take it in turns to be the leader. Granny and Aunt Florence are the audience. 'Amandla! Ngawethu!' means 'Power to the people!' Granny says that Dad would be proud of us.

Glossary

Apartheid is a system which separates South African people into four groups: White (about 4 500 000 people); Asian (about 800 000 people); African (about 21 400 000 people) and Coloured (which includes all the people not in the other three groups, about 2 500 000 people). Apartheid also separates the African people into ten groups, based on the languages which they speak.

The apartheid system was set up after white settlers from Holland, and later from Britain, had slowly taken over the land by force, during a period of over 200 years.

In South Africa, white people have many privileges which the other groups of people do not have. Africans are not allowed to vote for the government and make the laws.

In South Africa, there are some words which are used because of apartheid.

Homelands: In the early 1900s, the government set aside a number of areas and passed laws which said that African people must live only in these areas. Later, the government divided these areas into ten different groups which they called 'homelands'. African people do not use the word 'homelands'. Many people call these areas 'bantustans'.

The government divided the African people into ten groups, based on the different languages which were spoken. Each group was assigned to a different bantustan. KwaZulu is the bantustan for people who speak the Zulu language. African people are not allowed to move out of their bantustans to live or work, without special permission in their pass books.

Pass book: All Africans over the age of sixteen must carry a pass book. It contains a photograph of the person and says where they are allowed to live and work.

It is against the law for an African to be without a pass book, or to go to areas which are not in his pass book. These regulations are called the pass laws.

Resettlement: When Africans are forced to move from areas which the government has set aside for white people, they are resettled in camps in the bantustans.

Townships: These are usually areas on the outskirts of big cities. Most of the Africans who work in the cities must live in townships. No white people live in the townships.